A
DICTIONARY
OF
DISTINCTIONS

SECOND EDITION

DANISH AHMED

A Dictionary of Distinctions
by Danish Ahmed

Published by:
Ordinary Words Inc.
34 Woodrow Ave.
Toronto, ON M4C 5S2
www.ordinarywords.com

ISBN 0-9731360-0-6, print ed.

First printing 2000
Second printing 2002, completely revised

Cover and interior design and layout: Olena S. Sullivan

To my lovely wife, Mehnaz

Love & God Bless,

Donies John

CONTENTS

About the Author

Acknowledgements

Introduction – Dictionaries & Distinctions

Astronomy & Economics 1

Testimonials & Proof 3

Dream, Purpose & Mission 5

Common, Normal & Right 7

Force, Education & Example 11

Power, Influence & Persuasion 15

Think, Justify, Do & Feel 17

Truth, Belief & Reality 21

Manage, Lead, Coach & Mentor .23

Character & Maturity 27

Change & Progress 29

Prisoner & Slave 33

Balance & Integration 37

Respect, Support, Promotion & Edification 41

Independence, Dependence & Interdependence 45

Experience & Submission 49

Science & Technology 51

Respond, Act, React & Represent .53

Cost, Price, Purchase & Buy 57

Personal, Pervasive & Permanent .61

Decision, Preference, Interest & Commitment 54

Motivation & Inspiration 69

Principles, Practices & Truth 71

Negative & Wrong 75

Should & Could 77

Love & Trust 79

Happy, Joy & Enjoy 83

Attitude & Behavior 85

Intelligence & Wisdom 89

Promise & Guarantee 93

Dream & Fantasy 97

Giving & Contribution 99

Have To & Want To 103

Decide & Choose 105

Limit & Confine 109

Focus & Perspective 111

Poor, Poverty, Prosperity & Wealth 115

Simple & Easy 119

Conclusion & Finale 121

Upcoming Titles
Distinctions e-Zine

ABOUT THE AUTHOR

Danish (pronounced DAH-nish) Ahmed, a world-traveled professional speaker and coach, has been using and creating personal development material since the age of 15.

Over the years, Danish has enrolled himself into learning from every possible success coach. His experience includes programs by Dr. John Gray, Anthony Robbins, Dr. Wayne Dyer, Accelerated Learning, Stirling Institute of Relationships, Outward Bound, Up With People, the Sedona Method, Neuro-Linguistic Programming and network marketing. His keen interest in these areas, along with his personal interest in politics, dance, improv, spirituality and martial arts, has led him to travel around North America and to countries such as France, Hungary, Cuba, Russia, and Saudi Arabia.

Danish has accomplished many firsts. He was designing curricula and teaching by the time he was 16 years of age. He co-developed a revolutionary Internet technology that became the foundation of a dot-com startup. He has consulted with leading companies and has worked in the industries of stock market analysis, biotechnology, geographic information systems, and international trade. Although Danish's skill is technical, his passion is people so he continually seeks to integrate and implement peak performance technologies within himself, his family, his co-workers, and his community.

From visiting the White House on numerous occasions to getting married in Pakistan, Danish draws on his diversity of experiences to give *A Dictionary of Distinctions* a unique dose of wisdom that can't be found elsewhere.

Danish Ahmed is available by request for speaking engagements. You may contact him through e-mail at **danish@ordinarywords.com**.

Acknowledgments

Many people who contributed to the creation of this book should be acknowledged. First of all, I would like to acknowledge my family: my sisters Naz and Rahat for kindly proofreading and editing my initial manuscript, and the rest of my family for their ongoing encouragement and support. I would like to acknowledge my wife, Mehnaz, for bearing with me many late nights as I typed continuously and anxiously at the keyboard.

My circle of friends deserves acknowledgment for their faith and belief in my work. Such friends include Kevork Guerguerian, Andrei Losinski, Joseph Balderson and Dan King.

A couple of chapters in this book were actually written when I was in Estonia on an exchange program with Canada World Youth. I wrote a column called "Pump Up The Volume" for our local newsletter, *See On Newsletter* (the title means 'This is a Newsletter' in Estonian). Both my Estonian and Canadian friends deserve acknowledgment for reading the first versions of my work and for their tremendously valued compliments.

Over the years, I have participated in many youth parliaments. Ontario Youth Parliament and the Central Ontario Regional Parliament are worth mentioning because I feel they not only gave me an arena in which to practice my public speaking skills, but also helped me grow personally, socially, and spiritually in a time of my life when it was most needed. I recommend these organizations to anyone who fits the age requirements.

I would like to acknowledge DigiMap Data Services Inc. Not only do I have a nice group of friends at this company, but their support, respect and admiration certainly allowed me to persevere during the tough times. Thanks also to Michael Quinn, DigiMap's president, for providing me with a stable daytime income while I pursued my non-technical passions. Many authors don't have this unique and kind advantage.

I want to wholeheartedly acknowledge my up-line, Brad and Heather Fraser (an up-line is a person who sponsors or registers someone, directly or indirectly, into a network marketing business). Brad and Heather go out of their way to drive me, or to arrange car pools, so I can attend various business seminars and conferences. (Unfortunately, it's illegal to drive when you're legally blind.) Brad and Heather have done this for several years and continually do it without hesitation. Many of the seminars I wouldn't otherwise have been able to attend have either inspired me to write this book or have provided me with material I have used in this book.

Although I quote many authors, speakers or concepts from conferences and personal development programs, I obviously haven't included something from every book, tape or program I have experienced. This doesn't mean the experiences didn't bring value to my book. I know the energy and essence of all the programs I have participated in deserve acknowledgment because they too are helping this book become a success.

Nobody succeeds without a winning team of individuals all committed to a common cause. I've had the fortune to work with such a team. On my team is Harold Lass (harold.lass@sympatico.ca), who helped me set up and create my Web site. As a techie, I could have done all of this work on my own, but Raymond Aaron, co-author of *Chicken Soup for the Parent's Soul*, taught me to do only what I love. What a distinction! I'm doing what I love, but if I do only what I love, then of course I would hire someone like Harold to do the Web site for me. Harold focuses on what he's good at, and I focus on what I'm good at. That's what makes a winning team! (By the way, Harold was my grade nine English teacher and we have remained friends for the last 11 years!)

Two other very significant members of my team are my communications consultants, Denise Jetten (djet10@sympatico.ca) and Jennifer Tribe (jtribe@clearprose.com). Denise creates opportunities to generate as much public and media representation for me as possible and is always a great source of ideas. Jennifer has proofread this second edition and has also coordinated the graphic design of certain business and promotional materials. Together the three of us are synchronized in our thoughts and produce extraordinary results.

Finally, and most importantly, I would like to thank God. Without him, nothing is possible. And with me, all is possible. I thank God for giving me the idea for this book. I thank God for giving me the desire and persistence to write this book. I thank God for helping me to find a publisher. And I thank God for helping this book find you, the reader.

Introduction:
Dictionaries & Distinctions

A dictionary is a collection of words and definitions. Some dictionaries encompass the entire vocabulary of a particular language. Some dictionaries provide a translation of words from one language to another.

A distinction recognizes the difference between two ideas, facts, words or philosophies that appear, at first blush, to be the same or similar. When we realize the differences between words, we're more likely to use those words accurately and precisely in our working vocabulary. Two words that we once used interchangeably may now have whole new dimensions of meaning because of the distinctions we've discovered.

This book is a collection of distinctions between commonly used words. Rather than providing pure definitions, I have attempted to illustrate these distinctions by using examples. I have discovered these distinctions as I have lived my life over the last several years. They've made a difference to my understanding of the world. I hope they'll have a profound impact on your life as well.

By reading this book, I hope you'll increase the depth and scope of your communication skills, that you'll be able to see in language what you couldn't see before, create what you couldn't create, and most importantly, express what you couldn't express. And perhaps the next time you pick up a thesaurus, you'll be more conscious of the effect it can have on your vocabulary.

This dictionary may not seem that big when compared to say, the Oxford dictionary, but the words in this dictionary have been carefully chosen for their great power. Let me point out that the Lord's Prayer has 66 words, the Gettysburg address is 286 words, and there are 1,322 words in the Declaration of Independence. I won't dare to compare myself to these great works but I do want to point out the power a few words can have. I submit to you that by reading and understanding this book, you'll learn how to use words much more wisely.

Anthony Robbins says, "Nothing in life has any meaning except for the meaning we give it." I hope this book gives you the opportunity to generate further and deeper meaning from the words I have put forth. More importantly, I hope it gives you a deeper meaning in your overall life, making your life a "life of distinction."

PROMISES

I'll make a promise with you if you'll make a promise with me. I promise this book will change your life if you'll promise to read this book in its entirety. Promise you'll read it thoroughly and won't just skim through it. Promise you'll read it slowly and think about everything you read. Promise you'll read it several times over. Promise you'll try to extract all the positive aspects from it and won't try to compare my examples with personal examples of your own to find contradictions.

Yes, I know I'm asking a lot but look at what I'm promising. Many people will take the time and money to buy a book or attend a conference but few people will actually experience the book or conference in the same spirit with which it was purchased. Your first distinction starts here: Have you bought yourself *A Dictionary of Distinctions* or have you just bought yourself another book?

Many of the ideas within this book are my opinions. You may have a difference of opinion on some of the distinctions I illustrate. Nevertheless, I trust you'll benefit from my point of view and see that beauty and power come from the distinction itself. I sincerely hope we'll have an opportunity to communicate and compare our distinctions. I look forward to that time.

Astronomy

&

Economics

Paul Zane Pilzer is the author of *Unlimited Wealth* and one of my favorite speakers. He has helped me understand distinctions in economics and finance that have shaped my entire thinking. In one of his speeches, he illustrated the power a word's definition can have.

Before people believed that all the planets in our solar system revolved around the sun, people believed that all the planets revolved around the Earth. As inaccurate as our conception of an Earth-centric solar system was, we had an infinite amount of conviction that it was true. When astronomers attempted to disprove this theory with science and mathematics, they were laughed at and ridiculed, sometimes even excommunicated from the Church.

Perhaps one of the factors that made us believe so strongly in the false idea was our very language. The root of the word "astronomy" actually means "the study of planets revolving around the Earth." The very definition of the word limited people's ability to realize the truth. Fortunately, the definition of astronomy has evolved but it did take years of struggle to pull ourselves away from astronomy's literal definition. How many words do we use now that have meanings like this, words that by their very definition are "incorrect?"

Pilzer makes another very important word distinction. He says the word "economics" is subject to the very same limitations today as the word "astronomy" was many years ago. Open any textbook and it will quickly define economics as the "study of the distribution of scarce resources." However, most financially successful people will tell you there are no scarce resources. In fact, a resource only becomes a resource when a human mind develops a technology to use it as such.

True value in society can be generated from creating resources out of nothing. Look at some of the most successful people of the past 30 years: Ross Perot in data processing, Bill Gates in software, Fred Smith in distribution. In the industrial age, gaining control of natural resources created wealth. Think of J.D. Rockefeller and his oil fortune, for example. But we're now in the information age. Perot, Gates and Smith all made their wealth, not by controlling a resource, but by creating something completely new and allowing others to use it.

When people become leaders and start to teach others in society about distinctions, then society grows and excels. Pilzer is doing this in the area of economics. I hope I'm doing it more generally through this book. By changing our belief about a particular idea, we can grow outside the box. That growth could revolutionize society.

Maybe soon you'll write to me, telling me about another self-limiting word we use in our society. And maybe I can use your example in my next book.

TESTIMONIALS PROOF

"You always help me to see more of the spectrum. Your commitment to recognizing the truth and development in everyone is why I have amazing admiration for you."
- Andrei Losinski

Andrei is just one person. This book may have absolutely no benefit for you.

"I love it. Saying it from the heart, teaching us as you teach yourself, expressing without holding back. Thanks Danish."
- Steve Rogers

Who is Steve? He could be a completely fictitious character! Maybe he was someone who just got paid off.

"I admire your way of thinking."
- Naz Ahmed

Oh my God, a relative! Of course they would say something nice, you're thinking. I beg to differ. Getting an unsolicited, from-the-heart, authentic endorsement from any relative is a massive accomplishment. I'm surprised more people don't use them. I'm glad I do. Thanks Beast!

What's my point? We can prove mathematical equations all day long but we can't prove to each other whether something is worth reading, listening, or participating in. In order to push one another into making a decision to change, we often use social proof. Think of most advertisements that feature an average person telling you of their great experience with the product. It's crazy. Just because other people like something doesn't mean you will. I didn't want to take any chances though, so I included social proof as well. But hey, at least I tell you it's social proof! :)

Ultimately, the decision is yours. Will you make use of what you read in these pages or won't you? Dexter Yager, founder of Internet Service Corporation and the #1 network marketer in the world says, "Success is just a decision away."

You have come across this book because opportunity has knocked on your door. In his book *Opportunity Knocks*, Pat Mesiti says, "An environment of opportunity surrounds our lives. It's everywhere. Some people make a decision to act on it, while others make a decision to leave it."

To not decide is to decide, so you may as well make an assertive decision instead of falling prey to chance. If you need a further push, move your eyes back and read those endorsements again. :)

DREAM, PURPOSE MISSION

A dream is the visualization of a compelling future that sets your heart on fire.

Growing up, my dream was always to travel overseas to a foreign country. I thought it would be so magical and full of wonder. I had pictures in my mind of the scenery I would see, the people I would meet, and the culture I would experience. It was like that Disney song, *A Whole New World*!

Dexter Yager, the world's top network marketer, says, "When the dream is big enough, the facts don't count." The facts were I was still in high school, I didn't have much money saved, my parents didn't want me to go, and I had never been off the continent before. In fact, I had never been out of the country for more than a few days.

As a "techie" (a person with a technology background), I always thought the facts must count. Facts are facts. How can you ignore them?

I learned the facts can be altered. See, the fact is humans can't fly. The fact is there's this thing called gravity. Yet the Wright brothers had a dream that was bigger than the facts. They figured out how to use the facts to their advantage.

Without gravity, a plane can't fly. Gravity actually helps a plane fly in a specific direction towards a destination.

"When the dream is big enough, the facts don't count." My dream, thank God, was big enough. When I was 18, I headed off to Australia. What a beautiful country. I loved the fact I was living my dream, but I couldn't just bask in my glory and amazement for the six weeks of my stay. I needed more than a dream. I also needed a purpose.

A purpose gives you a sense of productivity and contribution as you carry out your day-to-day activities. It raises your level of self-esteem. In Australia, I developed a purpose to help other people. I volunteered at a community center with the purpose of helping people who didn't have families to feel better about their lives. As I cleaned cages in a local zoo, my purpose was to be cheerful while making the zoo a brighter, cleaner place. While tree planting, my purpose was to plant as many trees as I possibly could each day.

Something was missing, however. I didn't know what was missing but since necessity is the mother of invention, I soon discovered I needed a mission.

A mission gives you the drive to fulfill your short-term goals as you reach for a new long-term dream. In Australia, I was on a mission to acquire as many cultural distinctions as possible. I learned as much as I could about the native language, the geography, the education system, you name it. My mission was to assimilate this information so I could learn from it personally, and then teach it to others as I grew personally and professionally.

I'm glad to say my old dream was realized. Now it's time for me to conjure up a new dream, a new purpose, and a new mission.

Common, Normal Right

"The quality of your life is the quality of your communication." Change your communication and you change your life. When I heard those words from success coach Anthony Robbins, I knew they were accurate but I never dreamed how precise they were. Like most people, I think, I hear those words and translate them into something like, "I should be more positive."

In your day-to-day conversations, do you consider which of the three words – normal, common, and right – is most positive? The answer is none of them. None of them are negative either. But they all have a very different meaning. As a society, we've used thesauruses so much that we tend to group together words that may have very different meanings.

Rather than taking a lengthy course in linguistics, here is a quick course by example.

I was listening to an interview with Dr. Barbara DeAngelis, author of *How to Make Love All The Time* and an expert in the area of relationships, during which she was asked about divorce. The interviewer stated, "Divorce is normal – it's now over 50%!" Barbara wisely explained that divorce isn't normal. If you look at all of the civilizations throughout time, it's only in a very recent, very short period of time that divorce rates have risen so high. Marriage wasn't conceived so that people could get divorces. If the rate is over 50% today, that merely means divorce is common. Things can be common and not be normal. When we assume, through a consistent unwise use of vocabulary, that something is normal when it isn't normal, we actually create the statistics we all so fear.

Jim Jones, in a network marketing tape distributed by Internet Services Corporation, explains the story of David and Goliath. For 20 days, Goliath screamed over the hills for someone to challenge him. Each time he shouted, the people in the village became fearful and moved further away from his demanding voice. It was, and today still is, normal to be fearful – especially of such a vicious and giant monster like Goliath. However, was it right?

David decided it wasn't right. Even though he may have been motivated by riches, no future taxes, and the king's daughter, David was the only one who decided fear would be conquered by the right thing to do. David defeated Goliath.

Reading stories and anecdotes like these is common. We've seen these stories in all sorts of literature and always will. What is normal? Actually making use of the stories is normal. Putting them into action is normal. Unfortunately, while these things are normal, they're not common. Are you normal or are you lazy? Are you habituated with the routines that have always controlled you? Or are you willing to change?

If you're willing to change, then perhaps you're interested in moving to the next level, which is doing what's right. What is right? If you believe in an idea, then what's right is promoting it. The best way to successfully implement an idea is to educate other people about it. If you truly want the world to be a better place, start by sharing what you know is right. What you know may not be commonly known but it may be normal and it may even be right.

That's what this book is about: to share with love what I want my life to be about.

" Asking the right kind of question
is a skill that can transform
the way you think and
the way you get others to think. "

FORCE, EDUCATION & EXAMPLE

 The distinction between force, education and example came to me spontaneously, or spiritually, or energetically as I was sitting in a restaurant talking with my wife Mehnaz.

FORCE

Force is by far the quickest way to create change. It has the most impact but the impact is only temporary. Most people see the beauty of this way of change and abuse it. They forget that in order to use force, they must back it up with education and example.

EDUCATION

Education is the method of teaching a solid foundation of principles. Principles are timeless; they never change. That's why books like the Torah, Bible, and Qur'an can still make a massive difference in our lives today. By learning principles, we learn how to think. By learning how to think, we make the right decisions. Our actions are not changed by mere force but by biblical wisdom.

Example

In terms of change that lasts, example is the best method. It works the best over the long term because we, as humans, are not logical. No matter how much sense something makes, unless we see it evidenced in our lives we'll still choose to do the opposite. Having a hero you model your life after is very powerful because you're emotionally attached to making certain your habits emulate that which you've already decided is worth emulating.

The use of force, education and example as agents of change came up as Mehnaz and I were talking about children. (Let me note that having absolutely no experience in this area, I come from a purely theoretical point of view.) I said that hitting and disciplining children doesn't work. It only conditions them to feel negative emotions towards us, thus causing them to be even less open with us in the future. What we want to do is teach them how to make the right decisions.

The first part of teaching children is to listen. Listen to where they are and how they're feeling. Let them express themselves. Sometimes just by sharing they'll come up with the problems and solutions themselves. And maybe they'll be compelled to share even more with us in the future.

If we must ask questions, let's ask empowering questions. Did you like doing that? What did you like about it? (Everybody always likes something about what they just did.) How could you get that same feeling from doing something else? Ask and ye shall receive. Asking the right kind of question is a skill that can transform the way you think and the way you get others to think.

However, none of the love we teach will mean anything if we don't walk our talk. If we live a life that isn't consistent with our teachings, our children will notice. We must become role models to them. Ideally, I want our children to think of us as heroes. Most children today have rock stars or Hollywood celebrities as their heroes. If we live a life worth modeling, then our children will see us as heroes. That's the ultimate gift a parent can get.

I realize there's no magic method to causing or helping others to change. We must use all three methods of change in varying degrees based on the circumstances we're faced with. I think the nugget here is seeing the spectrum of choice we have, and not just resorting to what's easiest.

As I present or deliver this information to other audiences, I get some very interesting responses. Some people suggest other ways of being which are different than what I suggest. That's cool. But realize there's no magic bullet. I think that's why some people get discouraged with personal development material. They expect it to be the magic bullet. No. The purpose of this type of material is simply to help us open our eyes to things we haven't yet seen. If there were a magic bullet, one person would find it and saturate the market. Instead there are thousands and thousands of different types of material out there, and they all have some merit. I hope my material has helped you see a little more of the spectrum.

" Persuasion,
unlike power and influence,
is a bi-directional means
of change. "

POWER, INFLUENCE & PERSUASION

 Several years ago *Time Magazine* instilled within me a persuasive distinction between power and influence. One of their articles ranked the 20 most powerful people in the world, as well as the 20 most influential.

Bill Clinton was at the top of the power list. As an example of his power, the article noted how he could, with a simple signature, veto the efforts of hundreds of people working for many months in the Senate. Bill Gates, on the other hand, was voted the most influential person due to his ability to effect paradigm shifts in people's relationship to technology.

Authority, politics, and high status give you power but radical thinking, creativity, and drive give you influence. I propose adding a third alternative: persuasion.

Persuasion, unlike power and influence, is a bi-directional means of change. The one being persuaded is in communication with the persuader, possibly altering the content, type, or intent of the persuasion itself. Persuasion comes from people who are caring, open-minded, and wise. Persuasion comes from the Latin word "persuasio" which means "through sweetness."

All of us have powerful figures in our lives. Many of us have influential figures. Few of us have had a chance to be positively persuaded. Perhaps you had a caring teacher or counsellor who persuaded you to make a major decision in your life. Maybe you had a persuasive mother or father, rather than just a powerful and influential one.

During these times of mass mergers, you can be powerful like the large corporations who inflate commercialism, dominate markets and generate new profits. How about being influential by calling a television station and having them establish new guidelines so they're more politically correct in the future? Additionally, why not exercise the distinction of persuasion with random acts of kindness?

There are many means of change. The most prominent are logic, emotion, authority, and conditioning. Although various combinations are used, conditioning and authority work best for power, whereas logic works best for influence. Emotion works best for persuasion because it's about sharing touching moments, creating an emotional rapport, and creating an environment of complete honesty and trust.

Birdie Yager, arguably the top network marketer in the world, says happiness is:

1) Having something to do

2) Having something to look forward to

3) Having someone to love

Find the void that exists in other people and help them fill that void.

Think, Justify, Do Feel

 I was listening this morning to *The Magic of Thinking Big* by David J. Schwartz, Ph.D. Dr. Schwartz talked about "excusitous," the tendency in all of us to overuse excuses. We often make excuses based on our luck, age, smarts, talent and health. I was aware of most of these types of excuses, enough to know not to use them – except for the excuse of health.

I had been going through some nasty pain over the last week and had been using it as an excuse. Listening to *The Magic of Thinking Big* improved my whole day by helping me realize that no matter how much pain I was feeling, I could decide not to use it as an excuse to hold me back. As a result, I didn't feel the pain today.

Later in the day, listening to Anthony Robbins' tape on the six basic human needs was phenomenal. The first human need that Robbins identifies is the need for certainty; the second is the need for uncertainty. This appears contradictory but in fact isn't.

Robbins applies his concept to relationships to illustrate his point. We want to feel certain about the connection we have with someone. However, to continue to feel good, we also have a need for variety, whether it's emotional, mental, psychological or sexual variety. This is why, on a subconscious level, people who seem to be in a good relationship sometimes sabotage the relationship by creating arguments, cheating, or focusing on some other aspect of their life. The need for uncertainty has to be filled because it's a fundamental need of human existence, regardless of culture. I was on fire.

It was time to apply and test the theories. It was hard at first, as it always is, but it worked. I met with the millionaire next door, an acquaintance by the name of Steve.

Steve seemed to have it all figured out. He knew where he was in life, what he liked, and what he wanted to do, but he criticized the things I believed. For an hour, he attacked the basis of every personal development system on the market. He spoke from experience, having attended over 1,000 seminars and having met with the likes of Anthony Robbins; Dave Thomas, the founder of Wendy's; and Heather Reisman, CEO of Indigo Books & Music. He used both logic and reason to justify his position. When he was done, Steve pulled out a Harry Potter book and said that it, more than any of the personal development systems, was the best thing for him.

The axiom I had lived by throughout high school – that everybody is right because their experiences justify their reasoning – ran through my head. But for the first time I asked myself, "How can I feel good if I can't make a difference?" A sense of contribution is another basic human need.

I then arrived at the distinction for this chapter. At any moment, we can do anything, think anything, justify anything, and therefore feel anything. Most people go through a cycle where they feel, then think about how they feel, then act based on their feelings, and then justify the way they've acted. It all makes sense to them because, at the end of the day, they have justification behind them. Justification can be logical or emotional, but justification after action is a loser's excuse to be without control and to be a victim in life.

What we must decide to do is think about what we want, justify our thinking (we can never remove ourselves from justification), then act based on our thoughts, and finally feel based on our actions. If we're to be in charge, we must first decide (by thinking) how we want to eventually feel.

Losers: Feel → Think → Do → Justify

Winners: Think → Justify → Do → Feel

I thought about this. I justified it because it was time to write another chapter for all of you and help make myself feel better. I wrote it. Now I feel good. I got my sense of contribution after all.

We can decide what we want and how we want to feel. That's the ultimate goal of our lives: a consistent sense of pleasure within our being.

*“ Fear is having a belief,
a feeling of certainty, that the future will be
negative. Faith is having a belief, a feeling of
certainty, that the future will be gratifying. ”*

TRUTH, BELIEF REALITY

It was Albert Einstein who said imagination is more important than knowledge. But whether Einstein said it or not is actually irrelevant as long as I believe the statement to come from a profound source, and as long as I believe the statement to be valid. The source and the validity are what shape my actions, and therefore my feelings and emotions.

Let's take a look at how our mind works. We have beliefs that we form based on our values. Our values are formed from our past experiences, second-hand information, and the decisions we've made throughout our lives. In the leap between the past and the decisions we make today for tomorrow, lies the power of interpretation. We can interpret an experience as positive or negative based on our present mood, other environmental and biological factors, or pure randomness. How then do we strive for a consistent sense of pleasure within our being?

It was Anthony Robbins who said it doesn't matter whether a belief we hold is true or not. What matters is whether that belief empowers us or not. So really, it doesn't matter whether Robbins' statement is true or not. It matters whether it helps us to improve the quality of our lives. I submit to you that it certainly does.

When we find ourselves lost in a new culture, or at the end of our rope, knowing it wasn't our fault, that life was unfair to us, how can we persist? It's simple. Adopt the belief that it's a learning experience. Adopt the belief that there are new opportunities and optimism to be found from the situation. At the minimum, adopt the belief that this too shall pass.

When you can't adopt such beliefs, remember that faith and fear are polar opposites. Fear is having a belief, a feeling of certainty, that the future will be negative. Faith is having a belief, a feeling of certainty, that the future will be gratifying.

In the present, think of the beliefs that will help you in your moments of despair. Don't wait for the moments of hardship to practice this philosophy, for then it will be the most difficult. Practice now and in those difficult moments it will be second nature.

Empowering beliefs are as individualistic as the people who adopt them. You need not be an Albert Einstein or an Anthony Robbins. Remember Henry Ford's axiom of truth: "Whether you think you can, or whether you think you can't, you're right."

MANAGE, LEAD, COACH MENTOR

Political correctness is just upgraded terminology for the sensitive person's euphemisms. In extreme cases, affirmative action does create reverse discrimination. We lose vivid imagery when we lessen the power of our communication by softening our diction. Why not use this phenomenon to our advantage? Why not strengthen our communication by raising our standards?

The distinction between "manage" and "lead" should be obvious. Managers maintain, leaders progress. Do we want our society to stay where it's at, or do we want it to grow? Then why do we call some of our businessmen and women "managers?" Why not call them "leaders!"

Managers may do things right. That is, they will maintain the status quo because they'll do what has always been done. Leaders, on the other hand, do the right things. They have a sense of a greater purpose and mission to extend beyond their current abilities. Doing the right things may involve more risk but it will also yield a higher return.

Managers are usually efficient. They've learned to

streamline processes to get the job done as quickly as possible. Leaders, however, are more concerned with being effective. They have a bigger dream and vision in their minds than managers see. If leaders have to slow things down temporarily in order to speed things up in the long run, they will.

A coach is usually an outsider who isn't involved in the activities his trainees are involved in. This can be a great benefit. The coach is able to see things the players may not be able to see. The coach can share this information with the players, and by sharing some distinctions that only he can see from the outside, cause the players to win.

I hope that's what I am to you. I hope I can be a good coach who can share some distinctions to help you play a better game. Like other coaches, I may not be sharing with you anything revolutionary. But by sharing from the outside, I may be able to provide that unattached non-emotional leverage to help you push further ahead.

You may have already known the differences between a manager and a leader. But if you own a business, or if you're working for a company, how differently do you think you would feel with leaders instead of managers? You don't have to go around to every employee in the company and explain the distinction. The distinction can present itself subconsciously once the vocabulary is changed. That's the magic of words.

It's easier to be a leader with 100 subordinates than it is to be a leader in a group of three because a leader in a large organization has the law of averages and the power of momentum on his or her side. The law of averages says that in a group of 100, 10 people will follow the direction of a leader. The power of momentum will be illustrated as 10 more people follow the original 10, then 20 more follow, and so on.

In a smaller group, you need to decide to become a mentor. A mentor is a leader who has a specific person he or she wishes to train. A mentor creates a personal relationship with someone and allows that connection and intimacy to provide confidence and self-esteem to the one being mentored.

Dr. Gerald Janpolsky, who runs a chapter of the personal development system A Course In Miracles, says intimacy is "into-me-see." Intimacy is the magic a mentor can provide. By allowing others to truly see their heart and soul, mentors can foster trust. From trust, those that are being mentored can move forward, get outside of their comfort zone and eventually become mentors themselves.

Mentors are essential. We all need mentors to help us improve our lives. Professional speaker Mike Murdock says, "Experience is what God uses to teach fools unwilling to sit at the feet of a mentor." We'll find that mentors themselves have mentors. Having a mentor is an indication of future success. Mentorship is Gospel. Get a mentor and become a mentor.

"Many times you'll hear someone criticize a person by calling them immature, but how often have you heard someone say a person lacks character?"

CHARACTER MATURITY

 Maturity is acquired through diversity of experience. Character is acquired through intense amounts of struggle. Maturity is knowing what's right. Character is doing what's right.

By this definition, someone can be extremely mature yet have very little character. And, although it's less common, there are people with a lot of character but little maturity. The latter type of personality can be found in the young entrepreneur who has a lot of drive but not much experience behind it. I know, because at one time I fell into this category!

It's interesting that in the English language we have a word for a lack of maturity – immaturity – yet we don't have a word for lack of character. This identifies that we place a higher value on maturity than we do on character. Think about how people speak. Many times you'll hear someone criticize a person by calling them immature, but how often have you heard someone say a person lacks character?

What we should be doing is placing a higher value on character. We should acknowledge those who have character, and motivate those who don't possess it. If everyone had a solid foundational character then our society would function in complete integrity. What a world that would be!

The bad news is character does take struggle. If we can remember this during our times of hardship, our struggles will be more fulfilling and less frustrating. So when you've had one of those days where everything has gone wrong, where you lost a ton of money, annoyed a bunch of friends, or misplaced your valuable belongings, do as professional speaker Les Brown says: "Don't say I had a bad day today. Say I had a Character Building day."

Napoleon said, "The greatest single attribute of a leader isn't loyalty and it's not courage; it's endurance." Maturity will help you realize the importance of loyalty. Maturity will also help you realize the need for courage. Only character will get you through the tough times because only a strong character will stop you from giving up. Only a strong character will keep you persisting. And only a rock-solid character will keep you enduring.

CHANGE

PROGRESS

 People often look at successful people as being lucky. What these people are really doing is justifying their own failures with a classic demonstration of bad attitude. Sometimes people are not so bold or direct with their bad attitude. They camouflage their ignorance with statements like, "I don't have your talent," or "I could never present myself like you do," or "I just don't have your drive." I usually respond (if I'm in a good mood) with, "Yeah, but you could change."

Successful people are not born successful. Those who do get lucky usually lose their luck quickly. Look at all the lottery winners who lose their entire fortune only a few years after winning the jackpot. The bottom line (according to Dexter Yager) is, "Luck is a loser's excuse for a winner's commitment." We can also say luck is merely Labor Under Correct Knowledge.

I belong to a club called Toastmasters where we all take turns practicing our public speaking. One of my fellow Toastmasters once made a presentation where he outlined the possibility that change isn't necessarily good. For change to be beneficial, it must be progressive. For example, he said, e-mail and cell phones are a recent change in our society – but are they progressive?

He submitted they're not progressive because they clutter our lives and overwhelm us with unnecessary information. I agree with his reasoning. If e-mail and cell phones clutter our lives then they don't demonstrate progress for us. However, there are people out there who use e-mail and cell phones very effectively. There are people whose lives are enhanced by these technologies because they've learned to master their use. Without these technologies, in fact, many people wouldn't be able to do the business they're doing today.

Change will happen to all of us whether we want it or not. We must decide if it will transform into progress or whether it will debilitate our lives. We can learn to use e-mail effectively or fall prey to information overload. It's our choice.

There are some things we can't change. Steven Covey, the author of *The Seven Habits of Highly Effective People*, talks about our circle of influence. We can affect things within our circle of influence but beyond a certain point, it's impossible for us to create change. Realizing exactly where your circle exists is an art that will maximize your return on effort in life.

In Alcoholics Anonymous there's a saying that succinctly describes the circle of influence: God, grant me the serenity to accept the things I cannot change, the courage to change the things I can, and the wisdom to know the difference.

So maybe some people are right. They'll never be able to acquire certain talents. I know I'll never be a famous football player in the NFL. But I don't believe that those who are in the

NFL are lucky. Putting someone else down will never raise your self-image. There are more progressive ways to raise your self-image.

*"Anything in life can be a prison
and we can be enslaved by anything.
If it's time for a change,
start by changing the way you think."*

PRISONER & SLAVE

Dr. Deepak Chopra writes, "Change what you think and change who you are! It all begins with a single thought."

Prisoners know they're imprisoned. They think about how they can escape. They exert an effort to change. If they've been put in prison for a rightful reason, they question their actions and strive to change their attitudes. If they've been put in prison by malice, then they're committed to creating an escape plan.

Slaves, on the other hand, are usually conditioned to believe their way of life is normal. They seldom think about circumstances. They don't think about leaving their slavery. In fact, they justify their way of life. Slaves can't fathom anything outside of their own existence. If you attempt to take someone out of slavery, they'll probably rebel and fight you. They want what they know and what they're comfortable with. When Abraham Lincoln legally abolished slavery in the United States, many slaves chose to continue the way of life they knew as slaves!

These definitions don't apply just to those we traditionally think of as prisoners or slaves. Anything in life can be a prison and we can be enslaved by anything.

For example, do you believe you can have a life of financial prosperity? Do you believe you don't need a job? Can you see yourself living a life without waking up to an alarm clock every day? If you have a full-time job right now, and if you answered "yes" to the previous questions, then you might be a prisoner in your job. Right now, circumstances may be that you need a steady income from a reliable source. However, you're constantly looking for escapes. You're constantly intrigued by different opportunities that may come your way. You're always on the lookout for something better.

However, if you believe you'll work for the rest of your life, that only the lucky get rich, and that you'll never be free, then you might be a slave. You're a slave to an economic system that controls you. It determines when you wake up, where you spend your time, what you do, and how much time you can spend doing other things. Is that not slavery?

The sad part is this system of slavery will control your entire life until you die. The irony is if you're really a slave, you'll never believe these words. You'll be so caught up in the way you've been conditioned that you'll think I'm crazy. I can't help you there. It's hard to convince slaves to leave their slavery because they're so dependent on their way of living.

It's analogous to women who stay in destructive relationships. No matter how much you try to convince such a woman to leave, she has grown to consider a destructive relationship normal, and she won't leave.

You may think some women are trapped, with no way out, and that it isn't their fault. That's what the enslavers want the slaves to think, that there's no way out. The first step in escaping any slavery is believing there's a way out. There's always a way out.

I don't mean to beat up on anybody. There's actually nothing wrong with being a slave, just as there isn't anything wrong with being a prisoner. They're just two different ways of being. I've learned that in life, where we need to be is usually where we're at.

But if it's time for a change, start by changing the way you think. If you want to ponder more about this, think of slavery and imprisonment in all areas of your life: health, spirituality, relationships, business, family, emotions, time.

" No single element of our life can really be fully developed without developing other elements. "

Balance & Integration

I think professional speaking is a wonderful profession. All the speakers I know really walk their talk. They don't put a performance up on stage, they share their living up on stage. They're not perfect – nobody is. However, when you hear someone on stage then meet him or her off the stage and feel they haven't changed, you know they're a person of integrity.

How do they do this? I heard a voice mail message from MJ Michael, a successful leader in network marketing, that I believe sheds some light on how this is done. She described the difference between having a balanced life, and having a life that's properly integrated.

In our society, it's emphasized how everything in life is important. Our family is important and so are our finances, our spirituality, our health, our friends, our recreation. Society seems to think all of these elements need to be divided up relatively evenly. The theory seems to be that if you're spending five hours a week on your health, you should also be spending five hours a week on your spiritual life. While this does create a balance (an equal allocation of time) for each priority we may have in our lives, it also has a limiting presupposition.

It presupposes we're unable to combine different elements of our lives. Can we not go to the gym and work out with our friends? Can we not go to a financial investment seminar and spend quality time with our family? Is it possible to attend a worship service, socialize, and go out to dinner and a movie with friends from a religious community? You bet it is!

This is the process of really integrating our lives. It's realizing that no single element of our life can really be fully developed without developing other elements. It's realizing that different aspects of our lives don't need to be mutually exclusive. In fact, what a rewarding experience it is to share aspects of one area of our life with another area.

If you're a parent, why not sit down with your spouse and kids and actually do the household budgeting together? This gives you an opportunity to get a needed task done, spend quality time with those you love, and perhaps teach your children about proper financial management. The best way for your children to learn is through example. Why hide anything from them?

As you really integrate your life you'll gain many fringe benefits. In the previous example, for instance, you would probably learn more about budgeting by teaching your children. When you teach someone, you naturally learn more yourself. You might also learn where your children are in their understanding of money and wealth. You may even discover they can see distinctions you've never seen. This is merely one example!

It's all about maximizing our time. One of the quickest ways to get more time out of your life is to start playing audiotapes while you drive. Rather than listening to the radio all the time, buy yourself some good tape programs. They can be motivational programs, educational material, or even something as simple as learning a new language. When going on your next vacation to a foreign country, listen to a couple of tapes on learning the language. You'll be surprised how much better your vacation will be, and how much more you'll learn about the culture and people.

Here are some numbers that may inspire you. If you spend one hour a day driving to and from work, that adds up to 250 hours in a year. Assuming there are six hours in a school day, you'll experience 41 days, or more than eight weeks, of school. You don't have to go crazy and listen to a tape program every single minute you're in the car. But what if you did it 50% of the time? That's still a month's schooling over the course of a year. Why waste that time?

❝ *When we raise the image*
we hold of other people,
we naturally raise
our own self-image. **❞**

RESPECT, SUPPORT, PROMOTION EDIFICATION

 It's not that difficult to respect things and people. Our society almost puts too much emphasis on something we should do anyway. We should respect all things and all people. We should respect all beliefs and all ideas. Anything less than respect is arrogance. Frank Herbert says, "Respect for the truth comes close to being the basis for all morality."

Respect is a passive response. It's being disassociated. You can respect something, and never give it a second look or a second thought. You can respect a particular charitable cause all you want. Until you move to the phase of support, that charity will probably never see a cent from you.

Support is active. It's doing something and/or giving something. If you truly support a friend's business, then you're actively buying their products or services. To wish them the best of luck but not touch a product is almost disrespectful.

Support, by the very nature of the word, implies that we keep something from falling. While support may keep an idea from collapse, it certainly won't help it grow. True growth comes from promotion. Promotion is actively praising or endorsing an idea or service or product wherever relevant.

Unfortunately, with the mass media in our society, promotion has become taboo. We see so many advertisements all around us that whenever a friend tries to promote something to us, we think, "What's in it for them?" We believe that someone is always trying to sell us something.

Unlike advertisements in the media, genuine promotion isn't attached to a sale. When people promote something, they're just sharing what they've liked and would recommend. They don't have a hidden agenda to rip you off. And even if 1% of the population does want to rip you off, wouldn't it be better to go around in life thinking highly of people rather than living in fear of losing a couple of dollars? When we raise the image we hold of other people, we naturally raise our own self-image.

Edification is promotion at a higher level. We may promote ideas that entertain other people. We may promote products that save people time or money. We may even promote a seminar that will help improve someone's marriage. When we edify, we promote someone who will have a lasting effect on our entire life. We edify someone who has a purpose and a mission, someone who has integrity and someone who is interested in the betterment of our lives. We edify religious figures, strong business leaders, philanthropists, our parents and our heroes.

While the dictionary definition of edification may be restricted to "instruct and improve morally or intellectually," I, and many other leaders, believe the true definition goes beyond this. Edification is about sharing and transposing the trust and respect we have for someone to a third-party that may not know that person.

Holy books talk an awful lot about respecting our parents. I think the word 'respect' has been too loosely translated over the years. For example, the Qur'an gives examples of how we're to specifically respect our parents. We're to listen to them on every subject. We ought to make their lives easier. We should never disobey them. Even if they're wrong about something, we should honor them. We should always speak highly of them to others. These examples are more in line with edification. This doesn't mean we should be completely subservient to them. It's also a far cry from simply respecting them. It's proper edification. Isn't that what our parents deserve?

" If neither party came from a place of being

right, or being the authority,

or having the greater power,

and just came from a place of serving, what

would the results be? "

Independence, Dependence Interdependence

 Many people believe we live our lives in seven-year cycles. We live our first seven years as infants and young children. The second seven years are our years of puberty. Until the age of 21, we struggle through adolescence. The next seven years are those of courting and engagements, and so on.

As babies and children we're dependent on our parents for basic needs, such as food and protection. Through our teenage years we're dependent on our parents or guardians for shelter, support and education.

During our later teenage years, we strive to become adults. We believe adulthood means breaking away from a reliance on parents. We attempt to make our own money, make our own choices, and live as we wish. We seldom consider the advice of our parents.

Many of us succeed. We become independent. We find homes for ourselves. We find careers to carry us financially. We discover our own resourcefulness.

When we do settle down with that special someone, we may realize that being too dependent or too independent in the relationship isn't healthy. We may try to balance the two and think we've found the right combination, but what we must really do is integrate independence and dependence. We must learn to become interdependent.

Interdependence is when both (or all) people involved are dependent on each other. When we were children, we were dependent on our parents but our parents weren't dependent on us. In marriage, both spouses are dependent on each other. When we live marriages of true interdependence, we make our marriages last. When one person is too dependent or one person is too independent, then the marriage breaks down. There's a moving shift of power that's unhealthy and dangerous. Interdependence in marriage creates a solid foundation of mutual love and respect.

The concept of interdependence can be applied to our economy. When we create businesses that are too dependent on other businesses, they become vulnerable and can fail as soon as a supplier or customer decides to change. Businesses that are too independent can become large monopolies and control the social and cultural aspects of society. An economy needs to have healthy businesses that depend on each other. An economy of interdependent businesses will be well balanced and provide for everyone in the society. An economy of interdependence is the type of economy most likely to flourish.

The concept of interdependence can also be applied to an education system. Teachers who are too dependent on a government ministry to provide the details of their curriculum will be like robots who don't put any creativity or heart into their work. They won't have a passion for helping students excel in the ways students want to excel, but instead will be fixated on generating students who get high marks but don't understand a thing.

On the other hand, teachers who are too independent from a ministry or curriculum might let students slip from expected guidelines. In such a situation, it would be difficult to realize where a student stood in terms of the areas they're good in and where they need further development. Advancing through the grades could cause student confusion due to the wide variety of teaching styles and materials.

What if the ministry and the teachers were more dependent on each other? Wouldn't it be great if the ministry could provide a lenient framework for a curriculum that teachers could follow, and at the same time, teachers could provide constructive feedback on that curriculum? If neither party came from a place of being right, or being the authority, or having the greater power, and just came from a place of serving, what would the results be?

The concept of interdependence can be applied to just about anything. Use it. Dependence and independence are both too highly overrated.

"When you cease to set standards for the attitudes, beliefs, and conduct of your life, you automatically submit to those given to you."

EXPERIENCE SUBMISSION

An old playwright said it so well, albeit painfully: "There's love of course, and then there's life – its enemy."

Whatever stage we're at in life, we're always facing challenges and obstacles to our wants and desires. In Buddhism, it's taught that you can achieve true happiness when you cease to have any desires. The Landmark Forum tells us to have no expectations so that we shall never be disappointed. No matter how strong the battle, however, desire, expectation, disappointment and unhappiness will always be part of our lives.

To say such a thing isn't being negative. Buddhism, the Landmark Forum and other philosophies are all wonderful and true; subscribing to them is helpful. But remember that without light there's always what? Darkness.

Darkness is automatic; you don't have to work on it. When you cease to set standards for the attitudes, beliefs, and conduct of your life, you automatically submit to those given to you by social conditioning, glitzy high-paid marketing, and the intellectual candy found on the streets.

So at what point do we move from being a player in Shakespeare's tale "told by an idiot, full of sound and fury, signifying nothing" and rise to the level of freethinking architects of the future? To participate in a foreign exchange, to learn about a new culture, a new society, we must be willing to assimilate ourselves, if only temporarily, to get a real understanding of the lifestyle. Anything less than that level of commitment will gain us little more than the theoretical knowledge we can acquire from a textbook.

I don't have the answers, but asking such questions sometimes inspires abstract thought. A group of applicants to an exchange program were once asked, "What are you running away from?" Could it be it isn't so much the glamour of new adventures we strive for but rather a refuge from our day-to-day incompetencies? Or the simple notion of a back door? The idea that the length of this book is finite keeps us static.

The purpose of this book is to provoke thought and initiate positive change. Life isn't always simple but sometimes it's the simple things that keep us going. The next time you want to be safe rather than soaring, comfortable rather than commendable, remember that ships are safe in the harbor, but that's not what ships were built for.

SCIENCE
&
TECHNOLOGY

 I find it absurd how educational institutions group science and technology into one department. They're opposite ways of thinking.

Science involves using your imagination to generate a theory and testing it rigorously to establish a fact. Science is something of an art form because scientists create their hypotheses through inspiration, instinct and impulse more than through deductive reasoning.

A technology is simply a faster or better way of doing something you did before. Technologists use deductive reasoning, mathematical optimization and experience to create new methodologies.

Science usually deals with the chemical, biological, or physical dimensions whereas technology deals with the betterment of a scientific discovery, or the combination of different discoveries. For example, the ability to send signals through a cellular network is a scientific breakthrough. Creating cell phones that can send e-mail and surf the Web is a technological achievement.

How can you use this distinction? I'm not too sure – I'm a techie so I just find this fascinating! I guess what it exemplifies is the power society has to alter our perception of vocabulary. If everybody starts grouping the words "science" and "technology", then pretty soon we start ascribing the same meaning to the two words even though their meanings may be vastly different.

What other societal groupings of words may be misleading? Arts and entertainment? Business and finance? Leisure and recreation? Sports and fitness? Travel and getaways?

Our language is constantly shifting. How can we make sure it's actually progressing and not merely changing? Learn distinctions. Don't fall prey to classifications. Groupings and classifications will generalize your vocabulary. Our vocabulary should be very important to us because it determines our level of communication. And we already know that our ability to communicate (to others and to ourselves) determines our quality of life.

RESPOND, ACT, REACT & REPRESENT

Scott Michael, a prominent leader in network marketing, says, "Discouragement is a luxury you can't afford. So you have to move on. You can't react, you have to act."

Acting is deciding from scratch what you would like to do. It involves an overarching vision of where you want to go and what you must do. Reaction is simply acting out of a momentary condition. It isn't looking at the big picture. Reacting is short term and in the end, we often wish we hadn't reacted.

Between the lines of action and reaction lies the ability to respond. Responding takes into consideration your immediate conditions, along with the overall scheme of things, and is based on both short and long-term projections. Reaction is usually involuntary and may be dictated by automatic responses our bodies and minds have been conditioned with over the years. Responding is pre-meditative and requires thought before implementation.

When we extend the word "respond" we arrive at the word "responsibility." In fact, good responses should be considered responsible. That is, when we're responding to a given set of circumstances, we might want to have a sense of responsibility before providing a response.

For example, if someone asks us how we are, we can do one of many things. The most common behavior is reaction. "Good," we reply. We then carry on with our day.

Acting can be a lot of work. We may think about who this person is, who we are, what our relationship is, what we want to convey, how much we want to conceal, and so forth. Sometimes this is appropriate, especially when we're meeting someone very important for the first time. It's important to make a good first impression. We don't want to give old-fashioned responses or clichéd reactions, and we certainly don't want to look pushy or jump right into our life's details. On a first meeting, acting is very appropriate.

In most cases, responding is appropriate. When responding we might want to have a sense of responsibility. Think about how much of an impact you'll have on the person. Ask yourself how you want the other person to feel. In short encounters with acquaintances, you may simply want the other person to feel good. You may then choose to respond with something like, "I'm doing spectacular! How are you feeling today?"

Even when we're dealing with good friends, we want to have a sense of responsibility. When we're having a bad day, we don't want to dump all our negative thoughts and emotions on other people. How would you feel if you asked someone how they're doing and they answered, "Terrible! My back's hurting, I was late for work, and I can't stand my new co-worker!"

Having a sense of responsibility, we may decide to nourish a technique I call representation. Representation is a method of re-presenting our thoughts in a positive way. It isn't about being insincere. It's about being sensitized to a new, much more effective way of using our language.

When representing, we might answer, "Outstanding. I'm looking forward to getting together with you this weekend for dinner. Maybe you can help me with some health issues I'm dealing with. And I want to share some of the changes that are happening with me at my work place."

Make a decision to respond rather than react. Take on a powerful sense of responsibility. Re-present your thoughts and feelings into positive interpretations. Discover these distinctions and live a distinctive life.

“ Don't look at the price
of something and buy it,
look at the cost of something
and sell yourself on it. ”

COST, PRICE, PURCHASE BUY

 It boggles my mind how some people will drive around for 20 minutes in order to get something a few cents cheaper. They don't take into account that they've spent more money on gas and car depreciation than the money they've saved in obtaining the product. These people are looking at the price of a particular product. They aren't looking at the cost.

It's easy to look at the price of anything. If we know a little bit of mathematics, all we have to do is compare numbers on price tags given to us by the marketers. When comparing costs, we may have to do a little more arithmetic to compare product usage and consider other issues such as convenience, health, guarantee, etc.

Sometimes costs can be even more difficult to identify. For example, let's say you're presented with an opportunity to get into a business venture with a couple of your friends. The price of investment is $10,000. You decide the price is too high and you decline the opportunity. How much did that opportunity cost you? It may have cost you hundreds of thousands of dollars in possible income. It may have cost you a better lifestyle for you and your family. It may have cost your freedom. Think about the cost, not just the price.

Dolly Parton once said, "You'd be surprised how much it costs to look this cheap." We may think we're saving a bunch of money by wearing simpler clothing. However, if our image is important in our profession, how much is that decision costing us? We should never be fixated on price, only on cost.

We have and will purchase thousands of items in our lives. Purchasing is the simple act of exchanging currency for a good or service. Lots of people purchase all sorts of things they never use. Some people purchase educational material that lies dormant, collecting dust in their house. I also find the example of the fitness club amusing. Fitness clubs have a finite amount of space but always have an unlimited number of memberships available because they know when they sign us up that the probability of us coming regularly is slim.

When we truly buy something, we're actually sold on the product or service. To be sold on something is to make use of it as much as possible. When we're sold on the value of learning to use a computer, we don't just go out and purchase a system. We actively sit down in front of a screen and punch away until we learn something.

Usually we purchase tangible items. Usually we're sold on ideas, concepts or methods of improving our lives. When a salesperson gets us to believe in an idea, concept or method then they've truly made a sale. Moreover, depending on the product or service associated with your belief, the salesperson has probably hooked himself in for residual sales down the road. As you may or may not be aware, residual sales are the key to financial security.

Selling ourselves on things we need to do is a valuable skill. When we sell ourselves on something, we move ourselves towards consistent action. Don't look at the price of something and buy it, look at the cost of something and sell yourself on it.

" *Most of us do only the things we think we're able to do.* **"**

PERSONAL, PERVASIVE PERMANENT

If success is really simple – if you could go from being emotionally, financially and spiritually broke to being successful in all those areas – then why don't more people do it?

That's a question Anthony Robbins asks. I answer it with a saying from network marketer Scott Michael: "The will to win stems from the knowledge that you can win."

Most of us do only the things we think we're able to do. I'll give you an example. Before 1954, no one could break the four-minute mile because everyone thought it was impossible. But by 1957, after Roger Bannister had broken the four-minute mile, 16 other runners had also broken it. Today, people in high school are breaking it. Les Brown asks, "What changed? Gravity? The type of sneakers that people wear?" No, the will to win stems from the knowledge that you can win.

Let me illustrate a point about optimism. Dr. Norman Vincent Peale wrote a phenomenal book called *The Power of Positive Thinking*. We've all heard about the notion of positive thinking so many times that we generalize and demote its merits. We say, "I know I should be positive but being positive doesn't help me much." If it doesn't help us much, it's because we don't have the knowledge to use it. The will to win stems from the knowledge that you can win.

Psychologist Dr. Martin Seligmen from the University of Pennsylvania wrote a book called *Learned Optimism* that synthesizes the power of positive thinking into three basic steps.

1) Don't see a problem as being permanent.

2) Don't see a problem as being pervasive.

3) Don't see a problem as being personal.

I once came back from a trip a couple of months early because I had been removed from the travel program due to some misunderstandings. At first I saw the problem as being permanent. I felt I was unable to have any influence over the circumstances. Soon, however, I realized the trip was just one of many trips, I would have other times in my life to have better adventures, and the problem wasn't permanent. Being positive in and of itself didn't get me out of feeling down but knowing the first step – to be positive and not see a problem as permanent – gave me new hope for the future.

The will to win stems from the knowledge that you can win.

The second step was to not see the problem as pervasive, in other words, to not see it as affecting my whole life. At first I thought, what would my friends think, what would my family think? Will I be able to go back to Toronto and continue my career? Then I decided to think of the problem as not being pervasive. Sure, I had a challenge in one specific area of my life but it really had no bearing on my family, my friends, my work, or any other part of my life. My whole life wasn't screwed up. The problem was isolated.

The will to win stems from the knowledge that you can win.

Thirdly, I knew I had to see my problem as not being personal. Initially I felt it was my fault, that I was a bad person, that I always screwed things up, that I was undisciplined and weak. Then, remembering the key steps to optimism, I saw the problem as not being my fault. I may have made an error or two but so did other people. It was my responsibility to make things right, not blame myself.

The will to win stems from the knowledge that you can win.

It wasn't enough for me to "think positive." I needed a synthesized way of re-evaluating my thought process. Knowing what to do and knowing that I could do it, gave me the will to do it. It gave me the will to be positive. Such a distinction can transform a life of mediocrity into a life of excellence.

The will to win stems from the knowledge that you can win.

Abraham Lincoln said it isn't the outside world that will defeat you. It's what's inside your own borders. I hope I have given you a few tools to help you become more successful. Now it's up to you to make the shift from knowing what to do, to doing what you know. Take the "know" and turn it into will – the will to win.

66 When we truly make a decision,

we cut off any other possibility

except that which will generate

the results we've decided on. 99

DECISION, PREFERENCE, INTEREST COMMITMENT

Nobody wants to fail in life. All of us want to succeed. Sometimes, unfortunately, the difference truly lies in distinction.

Dexter Yager says, "Success is a decision backed up by a commitment." I then ask myself, "What is failure?" I say failure is a preference followed up with interest. It's noteworthy that in both scenarios, the objective is to be successful. People don't have preferences and interests because they want to fail – they have them because they truly want to succeed. Their lack of understanding is what holds them back.

Examples of preferences include self-talk like, "I'd love to win the lottery," or "I wish I could lose some weight," or "I want my relationship to improve." It's easy to have preferences. In general, all of us have the same preferences because all of us genetically want what's good and better for ourselves in life.

The word "decision" is derived from the Latin root "incision" which means to cut off from. When we truly make a decision, we cut off any other possibility except that which will generate the results we've decided on.

A good decision usually follows the same guidelines as SMART goals. That is, they're Specific, Measurable, Affirmative and action-oriented, Realistic, and Time sensitive/resource constrained. (For more about SMART goals, refer to *Goals and Goal Setting* by Larrie A. Rouillard.) "I'll make an additional $10,000 over the next six months," is an example of a SMART decision. It would then be wise to develop six one-month SMART goals to fulfill this decision.

An interest is just a preference on a larger, more practical scale. For example, we may have an interest in scuba diving, tennis, or playing the trumpet. I have interests in martial arts and jazz dancing. The interest allows me to practice these activities on a regular basis. However, if something else in my life comes up, I could easily forget about them. Interests don't have any level of priority. They can be postponed or canceled based on life's emergencies or our own procrastination.

A commitment is an interest with the highest priority. A commitment causes us to cancel or postpone other activities in our lives in order to fulfill it. We don't keep our commitments, our commitments keep us.

Let's suppose we're committed to reading 15 minutes every day. On one particular day we end up going to the hospital for a really bad headache. A person with a preference will use the bad day as an excuse not to read that day. A committed person will find a book somewhere in the hospital and read anyway.

Dr. Kenneth Blanchard, author of *The One Minute Manager*, makes a valuable distinction. It's OK to not be committed to everything in our life. In fact, we can't be. It's all right to have lots of interests. Similarly, it's also fine to state preferences. Not everything in our life has to be a powerful decision.

The power of distinction brings the understanding of what we're doing. When we do things by default, we're nothing more than stimulus and response creatures. When we state preferences by default, or when we have interests by default, we're just chess pieces someone else is playing. When we learn we have the power to choose, we can make a decision if it's appropriate, and we can make a commitment when it's the right time and place, then we rise above the mediocrity of life. We can influence the entire chess game. We become the mastermind.

66 We don't question the act of feeding our

physical bodies three times a day

but seldom do we make an effort

to feed our minds positive, motivating thoughts

on a regular basis. 99

MOTIVATION INSPIRATION

It's hard to write this book. I'm sure it's hard to write any book. Actually, it's hard to do just about anything worthwhile in life. So how do people do it?

Consistency. Drive. Determination. Passion. Fear. Desire. You've heard them all. They're all motivating factors. The word motivation comes from a Latin root meaning "move you to fly." Motivation pushes us to do things we might not otherwise do.

Zig Zigler was asked: "You pump people up. You motivate them. But how long does it actually last? Is it permanent?" Zig responded, "No, it isn't permanent. But neither is bathing." We don't question the act of feeding our physical bodies three times a day but seldom do we make an effort to feed our minds positive, motivating thoughts on a regular basis.

I couldn't get myself motivated today. Motivation derives from external factors. When motivations works, it's great, but our internal system and emotions will always fight external factors when they want to. That's how we might find ourselves in a place where we listen to a great tape or read a great book or talk to a loving friend but still feel terrible.

Don't worry, all the great speakers will tell you. They know how you feel; they've felt the same way. Here is what they've found: inspiration comes from within. Inspiration is something of a spiritual force that grows from within our being to get us to take action. Sometimes attending a great seminar or workshop can cause our inspirational abilities to be heightened but there's a secret to cultivating inspiration.

Consistent motivational input will create a habit of inspirational behavior. That's how I'm writing this now. All the motivation in the world couldn't get me to write tonight. However, all the motivational techniques I have adopted in the past and am committed to pursuing ignited a spark of inspiration within me to "just do it." I can't fully explain it but you're reading the evidence of it right now.

PRINCIPLES, PRACTICES TRUTH

 Practices are methods of doing a specific task. Ten Ways to Financial Prosperity, The A to Z of a Successful Marriage, and Goal Setting for Salesmen are all examples of practices. They tend to illustrate exercises and particular ways of conduct that will improve our performance. Practices are good because they give you the black-and-white of an issue. They're very timely and work very well for the time they're written.

A Dictionary of Distinctions isn't a book of practices. It's a book of principles. Principles are timeless; they don't change. They're pieces of wisdom we can apply to a vast array of situations. Great books like *How to Win Friends and Influence People* and *The Magic of Thinking Big* are principle-oriented books that are not only powerful today, but will be gems of wisdom in the years to come.

Although principles serve us far better, especially in the long run, there are several challenges with principles. The first is that principles can be oversimplified and taken for granted. Because they don't change over time, people often think they know them already. In actual fact, even though people may have already heard the principles, the wisdom gets watered down in their minds over the years.

If you saw a movie you liked several years ago, why would you ever see it again? Chances are when you do see it again, you enjoy it very much because you've forgotten many of the details. The same is true with principles of wisdom. If we don't consistently put the principles we know into everyday practice, we'll lose a lot of their benefit. Casey Comden, a successful network marketer and founder of InterBiz Business Systems, says, "To know and not to do, is not to know." That's a profound piece of wisdom. If you're not applying a principle, then you really don't know it.

The second challenge with principles is that we can't necessarily put them into immediate practice. With practices, you just follow a script, a text, or a model, and you instantly have a practice. How can you go out and apply a principle immediately? Principles need to sit in our minds and be fed different experiences. When we find ourselves in an experience that calls on a principle, we'll apply it. But if the principle isn't in our mind, or has not been in our mind for some period of time, we'll never realize the disadvantage we've given ourselves.

That's why I hope you don't read this book just once, but give it many reads. Once these distinctions start floating around in your mind, then you'll truly have opportunities to put them into action and benefit from them. A first read will only give you intellectual knowledge. A second or third read may give you some subconscious recall when you need it. Further reading will truly give you the ability to not only immediately recognize the distinctions I have presented, but to start discovering your own distinctions.

The good news about principles is that, unlike practices, they won't become obsolete. We get a lot more return on investment from learning principles. I define truth as something that's eternal. In other words, for something to be true, it must have been true yesterday, must be true today, and must still be true tomorrow. That's what a principle is. A principle is truth.

So many love songs say "... and the truth is ..." I used to wonder why people would put in so many filler words. What do those words really add to a song or romantic poetry? Are we not supposed to speak the truth all the time? Well, if you apply my definition of truth then the line does add a lot to the meaning of a song.

" *Let's believe no one*
does anything 'wrong',
but that people simply behave
in ways that don't agree with us. **"**

NEGATIVE & WRONG

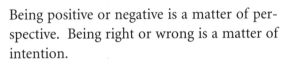Being positive or negative is a matter of perspective. Being right or wrong is a matter of intention.

One of the things the Landmark Forum teaches is not to make other people wrong. I think this is a powerful understanding to adopt. Let's go along in our lives always assuming that whatever other people have done, however bad it may seem, that their intentions were well founded. Let's believe no one does anything "wrong", but that people simply behave in ways that don't agree with us.

Trusting intentions is pivotal in any relationship. Whenever our partner does anything that doesn't please us, we should try to remember their intentions were probably good and they meant well. As soon as we start to question the other person's intentions, we question the integrity of the other person. By extension, we question the integrity of the very relationship itself. Question people's behavior all day long but never question their intentions.

Everyone can be right and still be negative. Our mother can say to us, "Why don't you ever wear your sweater when you go out in cold weather?!" Her tone may be harsh, and she may not understand your reasons for leaving your sweater behind, but her intentions are very loving. She wants you to be warm and safe.

There are times when being negative is very appropriate and beneficial. For example, if you're a doctor performing heart surgery, you want to be negative in your preparation. You want to think about all the things you need, and you want to check your list twice. You want to think about all the things that could possibly go wrong and make sure they don't. You want to be positive about your performance and your outcome, but negative in your execution. Being negative in this situation could mean the difference between life and death.

Many people mistakenly believe Dr. Norman Vincent Peale's message about the power of positive thinking means we must be positive 100% of our lives. There are times when being negative is the right thing to do. What Dr. Peale tried to emphasize, though, is that negative thinking happens by default. We as human beings tend to think negatively. It follows that we should put more of our energy on trying to be positive.

Balance is believing we need to be positive 50% of the time and negative 50% of the time. However, when we realize being negative is automatic for us and we'll do it without thinking, we need to learn that we should exert energy in being positive 95% of the time and negative 5% of the time. That's how real balance might be achieved.

SHOULD
&
COULD

 About six years ago, I attended a phenome-
nal week-long leadership course by Robert
Hoey while visiting southern Australia. One
of the distinctions Hoey introduced me to
dealt with the words "should" and "could."
To this day I haven't heard or read anything else that talks
about this distinction.

It's true that as you make a habit of reading positive books,
listening to motivational cassettes, and attending life-changing
seminars, you start to hear some of the same things. Don't use
this as an excuse to stop learning. Repetition is helpful and
you'll also find some rare and unique nuggets. I'm surprised
no one else has emphasized the distinction between "should"
and "could" so I'll present it to you now.

"Could" implies possibility. We could read positive books
for 15 minutes every day. This opens a door to opportunity. It
implies we have choice and we'll ultimately decide what we
want to do.

"Should" implies obligation. When we use the word
"should," we imply a sense of what's wrong and what's right.
We should read positive books for 15 minutes every day. This
statement, as helpful and effective as it may be to some people,

can shut some people out. It can be damaging to people who don't yet read 15 minutes every day. They may feel a sense of superiority coming from those of us who do read daily, and it may lower their self-esteem.

Next time you have a beef with someone, instead of saying, "You should be more sensitive," try saying, "You could be more sensitive." You'll be surprised what a difference a word can make. The word "could" will actually open a door to the person being responsive and asking for solutions. They might reply, "What will make me more sensitive to you?" instead of responding to a perceived insult with one of their own ("Well, you're not very sensitive either!").

Be sensitive. Use "coulds" more often.

And don't have too many "shoulds" in your life. They create too much pressure. Imagine how you would feel if you thought you *should* be a perfect spouse, you *should* be a great professional, you *should* be a loyal friend, and you *should* be in terrific health. Don't "should" all over yourself! We *could* be all of these things. When we can be, we're more likely to be.

LOVE
&
TRUST

Some people think all sorts of words are synonymous with love. Words like devotion, money, understanding and support. I guess some people really do think love is all things to all people. American author Diane Ackerman says, "Everyone admits that love is wonderful and necessary, yet no one agrees on just what it is." Anthony Robbins says love is the most sought after commodity in human experience.

Trust is very important in any relationship. The more trust we have in a relationship the healthier that relationship will become. It's important to understand, however, that a lack of trust doesn't mean a lack of love. For example, we may unconditionally love our eight-year-old son. We may want the world for him and do anything we can for him. But would we trust him to drive us to the grocery store? I don't think so.

Trust is based on intelligence and experience. Our intelligence tells us an eight-year-old shouldn't be driving a car. Our experience tells us allowing an eight-year-old to perform such a task would prove disastrous. When the child grows up, will he appreciate the fact you loved him so much you allowed him to drive your car? He won't. Too much trust can actually destroy the love for which it was intended.

Because trust is based on experience, it's very easy for someone to increase the level of trust others may be giving them. Rather than complaining that someone we love doesn't trust us enough, let's try to conduct ourselves so we gain more of their trust. Take on that responsibility. And when someone demonstrates higher levels of responsibility, let's grant them more trust, for they deserve it.

In a loving relationship, or in most relationships, trust shouldn't start off at zero either. At a minimum, we could trust that the people we're in a relationship with are coming from a place of good intentions. Sure, there might be a small percentage of people out there who are conniving and who will take advantage of our trust. I would rather fall prey to this small percentage of people than ruin my chances of very fulfilling relationships with hundreds of other people.

Remember, we can justify anything. If we look for examples in our lives where people have abused us or ripped us off, we'll find them. Does that mean most people are cruel and untrustworthy? If we look for times in our lives when people have been kind, considerate, and very helpful, we'll find those examples too. Does that mean most people are good people and should be befriended immediately?

What's true is whatever we decide to make true in our minds. Find experiences that help you to justify loving everyone. Find experiences that help you give everyone a good starting point of trust, but also help you be cautious enough not to get burned. That's a good place to begin very fulfilling relationships. We never know when and where the next beautiful relationship we're going to experience will be generated.

I wish you tons of love. And I wish you the right amount of trust to generate that love.

❝Happiness is attained
when we take our focus
off happiness and put it
on helping other people.**❞**

Happy, Joy
&
Enjoy

 Abraham Lincoln said, "People are as happy as they make up their minds to be." I don't think people decide one day they're going to be happy, but they do continuously seek it. In fact, the inalienable rights granted in the Declaration of Independence are life, liberty and the pursuit of happiness.

I believe happiness is a by-product. You can't chase after a by-product. You must seek out the product that creates the by-product. Money is also a by-product. You only attain true wealth through adding value to society. Once we stop focusing on financial possessions and focus on adding value, we automatically get riches.

Similarly, happiness is attained when we take our focus off happiness and put it on helping other people. Zig Zigler, in his program *Over the Top*, says to get what you want in life you just need to help enough other people get what they want.

If you read the Bible, you'll notice it rarely mentions happiness. However, you'll also notice it mentions joy quite often. That's the wisdom of the book. Being joyful is having the ability to create a sense of optimism or enthusiasm from within.

In fact, the word enthusiasm means "God within." We have the power to be joyful because we can decide in any circumstance to put on a happy face. We do have that power and we do have that choice.

Being joyful does not necessarily make us happy, at least not right away. That's where most people get frustrated and give up. They say to themselves, "Being joyful isn't working. Why even bother? I don't want to be a fake!" What they don't realize is that being joyful *is* working. It just takes time. Try to be joyful for 10 days in a row and then ask yourself if you've had a happier week than you normally do. Unfortunately, we've all become accustomed to instant gratification, so much so that we seldom have the patience to truly try anything new that doesn't have microwave-oven turnaround time.

So the next time someone asks whether you're *enjoying* yourself, and you answer no, just remember you made that decision. Enjoyment doesn't come from the outside, it comes from the inside. In any situation, you can be enjoying yourself. Again, that doesn't mean you're happy or are having a marvelous time. It does mean you're willing to put out enough positive energy to fight off what may be negative energy all around you. What a wonderful world it would be if everybody did that daily.

ATTITUDE & BEHAVIOR

 Zig Zigler says it's your attitude, not your aptitude, that determines your altitude in life. While I wholeheartedly agree with this statement, I think most personal development systems don't emphasize that we have just as much power through our behaviors as through our attitudes.

It isn't what happens to us in life, it's how we handle it that matters. When something doesn't go the way we'd like, let's change our attitude. By changing our attitude, we can focus on what we do like. We can find the positive in what has happened. We can learn from our mistakes. We can discover humor in the situation. We can decide to change the situation. We can commit to not ever allowing those circumstances to happen again. All that's possible simply through our attitude. Motivational speaker Dennis S. Brown says, "The only difference between a good day and a bad day is your attitude."

Sometimes we feel so badly that we simply don't have the energy to change our attitude. Or we just don't care to. Changing our attitude takes work. Until it's a fully developed habit, it can be very difficult to discipline ourselves to make the change. That's when changing our behavior can be just as fruitful as changing our attitude.

Changing our behavior may involve something as simple as changing our physiology. We can stand taller, look up, smile, move rapidly, make powerful gestures, talk about something we're passionate about, or exercise. These techniques take a relatively small amount of effort, and we don't have to think about them like we do our attitude. We can simply do them.

Actions do speak louder than words. Changing our actions will automatically change our thoughts. Changing our thoughts will automatically change our attitude. At the very least, it will give our brain enough empty space and will power to change our attitude.

We all want to change the way we feel at times. Changing our attitude is one great way. Changing our behavior is another way. In fact, these two methods influence each other. Often, changing our attitude will change our behavior and vice versa. When we're able and willing to change both, the more power to us!

Here's a tip. Try using the bi-directional force between attitude and behavior with children. For example, when a child is misbehaving, get them to focus on their attitude. If a child is taking something that doesn't belong to them, don't just scold them and tell them it's the wrong thing to do. Ask them what they're thinking. Find out what their values and beliefs are. Get them to look at the situation from another perspective, maybe even a humorous perspective.

If a child has a bad attitude, get them to change their behavior. For instance, if a child is being stubborn, request that they stand up straight. Get them to do 25 jumping jacks.

Tickle them until they start laughing. Now see if they're still as stubborn.

As we try out some of these strategies – whether it be with kids, our friends, or our co-workers – we'll find we're much more likely to try them out on ourselves. Go for it!

" We don't need a long beard

to be wise. "

Intelligence Wisdom

Many people think they know the difference between intelligence and wisdom. So here is the first distinction between these two words: Wise people will still read this section eagerly whereas simply intelligent people will skim right through it. Wisdom is associated with humility. Intelligence is associated with pride.

A wise person is always seeking new knowledge. An intelligent person is always telling people how smart he or she is. Intelligence is gathering facts, knowledge and know-how into one's mind. Wisdom is sitting back and pulling a few key principles from that base of information. Intelligence is sharing the quantity of data you have. Wisdom is pulling out the right pieces at the right time.

There's nothing wrong with intelligence. In fact, we need a certain amount of intelligence before we can get anywhere near wisdom. On the other hand, don't just sit around collecting intelligence waiting for wisdom to pop into your mind one day. Wisdom doesn't come solely from experience but also from perspective.

Intelligent people may take something simple and make it seem more complex. Wise people will take something complex and make it simple. They understand that simplifying things for others is what creates understanding and moves us forward. They have perspective. They can see a situation from many sides. They don't judge. They perceive. They learn as they teach and they teach from the heart.

"Geeks" have an interesting place in our society. Usually people don't like being around geeks. Geeks are very intelligent and can always teach us something, so why do we run from them? It's because these people tend to share everything they know all the time to all people. They don't understand there's a time and place for everything. They're so caught up in teaching and learning that they miss one of the most important principles in life: adjust to your environment.

Those who are wise understand this principle perfectly. When they're in a crowd of salesmen, they seem to share a lot about sales. When they're with their family, they seem very caring and loving. When they're at a business function, they share all sorts of knowledge they've recently acquired. When they're out with their significant other, they're just focused on having fun. That's why society doesn't like being around geeks but loves being around people who are wise.

Professional speaker Mike Murdock says, "Wisdom is God's laws applied accurately." All of the Holy Books are full of wisdom, not intelligence. One of the beautiful things about wisdom is that we can re-read a particular scripture we've read a hundred times before, and on the 101st reading, discover yet another piece of ancient wisdom.

We don't need a long beard to be wise. We just need to keep perspective on everything. Look at situations from all sides. Be open-minded. See the big picture in things. Read wisdom-filled books. Soon you'll have future heroes crossing your path, asking you for guidance. What a rewarding experience that will be.

" One of the ways to grow

is to bring the concept

of a solid promise

back into our economy."

PROMISE

GUARANTEE

 Many consumers want the products they buy to have a good guarantee. I would prefer to get an authentic promise from the vendor.

Unfortunately, guarantees have more legal weight than promises. A guarantee gives you a sense of security, but doesn't really move you forward. For example, a guarantee may state that the buyer of a defective product will get a full refund. As consumers, we then know we won't lose our money. That's security. But do we really move forward? We don't want to exchange our money for a bad product and then exchange the bad product for our money. That's just a big hassle, and that's why guarantees are losing the strength they once had.

A promise has more of a personal ring to it. If someone breaks their promise, it's a terrible thing! Most people will do anything to keep their promises, in fact, that's what a promise means. There's no security because if someone breaks their promise, we don't necessarily have any legal recourse against them. On the other hand, except with crooked businesspeople, there's more authenticity.

A vendor of a product may not take good care of it if he or she relies on the guarantee of the manufacturer to cover any loss or damage. However, if the vendors themselves are providing a person with a product and promise, they're much more likely to take personal care of the product to ensure its fine delivery to the customer. Especially in cases where you have a long-term relationship with a vendor, or know the vendor personally, you may consider asking for a promise rather than a guarantee.

Long ago, when our economy was in the business of bartering things back and forth, there were implied trust, respect, and promises between merchants. There had to be in order to have that type of economy. Now, we find ourselves in times of acceleration and growth thanks to currency and electronic transactions. But that doesn't mean we have to completely lose our notions of trust and promise. One of the ways to grow is to bring the concept of a solid promise back into our economy.

One of the events that helped me discover the importance of this distinction occurred while I was working at a technology startup. We had to devise a privacy statement for our Web site. Typically, sites title this section "privacy policy." Our Chief Executive Officer decided to use a stronger headline. He wanted to call ours a "privacy promise."

I thought about that and realized what a significant difference a simple change had made. Would you not trust a Web site far more if they had a privacy promise instead of a privacy policy? It's easy for policies to be changed and manipulated but you have to be a pretty immoral person to do that with a promise. What's more, everyone else will see you as an immoral person if you tamper with the promise.

Become a person of integrity. Make promises with others. Make more promises with yourself. And never, ever break any promises. I promise you, you won't regret it.

" They say a picture is worth

a thousand words.

If so, how much is

a five-minute dream worth? "

DREAM
&
FANTASY

 Scott Michael says, "If you don't have a dream, how are you going to make a dream come true?" Dreams inspire us. We all want our dreams to come true. We all need dreams to drive us to growing levels of achievement in all areas of our lives.

Why do dreams have a negative connotation for some people? I hear some people say with a funny smirk, "Stop daydreaming." Daydreaming is a powerful tool we all possess. We can't necessarily control our dreams when we sleep at night, but we can control our daydreams. When we can focus our dreams on the things we want out of life, we can massively influence our future. We're deliberately telling our subconscious mind what we want to do, where we want to be, and who we want to become. That's powerful.

Bill Gates was asked what he thought the formula for success was. Bill stated:

1) Be at the right place at the right time

2) Have a vision of what's possible and what will be

3) Take massive and immediate action

Realize that vision is the first step towards having a dream. A vision creates an image in our mind of what things can and will be. A dream takes that picture and makes it into a full-motion video. It adds sounds, dimension, feeling and life. They say a picture is worth a thousand words. If so, how much is a five-minute dream worth? Millions.

At the time the Epcot Center was being built in Florida, a reporter commented to a Disney executive, "Too bad Walt didn't live to see his creation." The executive replied, "Walt saw it before you and I did. That's how it stands before you today." That's the power of vision and dreams.

A fantasy, on the other hand, is unrealistic. It's a dream that won't come true. Many times, if you ask someone to state whether a certain scenario is a dream or a fantasy, they'll choose correctly. Yet if we ask them what criteria they used as the basis for their decision, they'll be at a loss for words. A dream is realistic, a fantasy isn't. But what makes something realistic or not?

I think the answer is that we can intuitively pick out what's immoral and what lacks integrity. I think we find that most fantasies are either unethical or don't have a foundation of solid character. Fantasies glorify the consumption of wealth, power, status, love, and other types of gratification. Dreams focus on giving, growing, and participating in something greater than we are.

Although dreams and fantasies are distinct, a particular vision may transition itself back and forth. You may find a dream that migrates its way into a fantasy. The good news is that you have the power to transform a fantasy into a legitimate dream.

Visualize, envision, and dream. Dream big dreams. One day they will come true.

GIVING

CONTRIBUTION

 In a past Successories catalog, I noticed a wonderful saying: "You make a living out of what you get; you make a life out of what you give." I think those are powerful words. I also think that some quotations use words that fit in order to accomplish linguistic ingenuity, rather than choosing words that are precise for the intended meaning.

While it's important to give in life, giving is usually centered on money or physical goods. While giving isn't the easiest thing for us to do, it certainly isn't the hardest. If we don't live in absolute poverty, we always have something to give. In fact, all the major religions focus on the importance of giving. The beauty is, the more we give, the more we get in life. It's a force that many can't explain. We can't trick this force by giving with the expectation of getting something in return, but if we give unconditionally, the forces of nature will automatically give us abundance in return.

Anthony Robbins explains it this way: if we condition our mind to give, what we're teaching our subconscious is that we have abundance. When our mind believes we have abundance, we live our life abundantly. And when we live our life abundantly, more money and people are attracted to us. If we live in scarcity, nothing is attracted to us.

Contribution is something more than simply giving. It's a sense of being interactive. Usually people contribute time, energy, effort, ideas and possibility. Notice that when we give, we usually give something very tangible. Contributing isn't necessarily tangible but it's very qualitative. Contributing a bit of time and energy to develop a plan for a charity can translate into millions of dollars of value. Contributing a bad idea can actually result in a loss for the charitable organization.

In order to contribute, or make a qualitative impression, we must be people of quality ourselves. Anybody can give money, but those who contribute need to have more. Perhaps it's heart. Maybe it's passion. How about a strong character foundation? A "bad" person can't contribute to any organization in the world. He or she will soon be found out and asked to leave. We must be good people before we can effectively contribute.

Contribution also has another fringe benefit. It causes us to grow personally. More often than not, we learn tremendously from the experience. We not only feel good about our deed, but we may get warm hands, little smiles, or the satisfaction of seeing our contribution produce immediate results. Sometimes contributing has a very residual effect. Years after we contribute to a certain cause, we may still have people thanking us for our contribution.

I decided a couple of years ago to act as a volunteer coordinator for the International Storytelling Festival. It was an incredible experience. I learned how to recruit people. I fostered my skills in working with a wide range of personalities. I gained knowledge in how to stage a large-scale festival. And I had lots of fun. I got more out of the experience than I could ever have imagined.

Had I applied for a job with similar responsibilities, I would not have been hired. I had never told a story before in my life and I certainly had never managed a group of 25 people. My volunteer experience helped me perform better at my job and to discover some other things I really enjoyed doing.

Give yourself the gift of contribution. It can change your life.

" *It's always a good idea to ask*
yourself whether you really
have to do something.
You may be surprised at some of the ideas
you'll come up with. **"**

HAVE TO
&
WANT TO

 You might read the heading of this chapter and think you know the difference between these two terms. Do you? More importantly, do you apply them accordingly? Casey Comden says, "To know and not to do, is not to know."

Sometimes people complain about their jobs. (Well, more than sometimes.) But if you ask them, "Then why are you working there?" they respond, "Because I have to." No, you don't have to! Not in this country, anyway. You don't have to work at that particular location, at that particular company, in that particular neighborhood or province or state. Bo Short, a professional speaker and successful international network marketer, says, "You live in the greatest, freest country in the world. Now do something with your life!"

We have so many choices in our lives that we take everything for granted. We become complacent. We tend to associate "have to" with things that are habits for us, things that we've been conditioned to. It's always a good idea to ask yourself whether you *really* have to do something. You may be surprised at some of the ideas you'll come up with. Sometimes asking the right question can cure a bad habit.

On the flip side of the coin, it's a good idea to say "have to" where we might say "want to." When we make a commitment to lose weight for example, and somebody asks us why we're not eating dessert, don't answer with, "I want to lose weight." When we tell our brain we want to do something, our brain automatically finds a back door and tries to escape the pain it feels.

Why not say, "I have to lost weight!" or "I must lose weight!" What's even better is to prepare answers to the natural questions some people may ask.

"Why do you have to lose weight?"

"Because if I don't, I won't be able to fit into the wonderful dress I want to wear when I go out with my spouse for a glamorous dinner next month." "Because if I don't, I'm going to start being so unattractive it will affect my productivity at work." "Because if I don't, I'm liable to have some health challenges my doctor told me about."

Imagine what a difference such responses would make to our brain and therefore our actions. We'll never even be tempted by dessert because our mind will already have solid reasons as to why we "have to" lose weight. And there will be no back doors.

Changing the places we use "have to" and "want to" can have a profound difference in our lives. Remember, the way we communicate to ourselves (the talk we have inside our head that no one else can hear) is far more important than the way we communicate with other people.

DECIDE
&
CHOOSE

 For much of my life, I have hated reading. I was a good reader in elementary school but I guess because my eyes were in so much pain from reading small print (I'm visually impaired), I tried to stay away from it. I plagiarized many of the book reviews I submitted in high school, or I squeaked by reading condensed versions and study aids.

As I started getting involved in personal development, I had a huge inner conflict to deal with. Much of the personal development material I listened to on tape or heard at conferences would say things like "leaders are readers." The speakers insisted that all successful people read daily. How could I subscribe to just about everything my role models were telling me except for this one, very important, issue?

I tried. Boy, did I try. I would sit down and start reading. Thoughts would go through my head like, "I already know all of this." Or sometimes I thought, "This guy has said the same thing 10 times. I could sum this book up in one sentence!" But my personal favorite (in retrospect) is, "Any idiot can be an author of this crap."

Decisions are powerful, as I discussed in an earlier chapter, but sometimes we need to do more than decide. We often use logic to make a decision. I used logic. I knew I should read. I knew it would benefit me. I knew I couldn't be a hypocrite. I decided myself into reading, and my mind decided myself out while I was trying to read.

Jerry Meadows, a professional speaker and successful network marketer, made an amazing comment I heard recently. He said we don't make any decisions based on logic. All our decisions are based strictly on emotion. We may try to justify our decisions through logic, but ultimately, those decisions are made by emotion. That's a very bold concept – bold and accurate.

I knew I couldn't get myself to read because my emotions just weren't there. Making a decision wasn't powerful enough. Then I remembered a distinction I heard through Landmark Forum.

The Landmark Forum teaches that choice has nothing to do with logic, emotion, consideration, benefit, convenience, or anything else. Choice is simply choice. We choose because we choose. That's one of the hardest distinctions to understand, especially if you haven't done the Forum. I recommend you go out and register yourself today.

Today, I'm choosing to read at least 15 minutes a day. There's no logic behind it. There's no decision behind it. I don't do it for a particular reason. I do it because I do it. I choose to read.

I might justify it by saying I become a better person by reading daily. I might justify it by telling people all the great things I learn and how much I grow daily. But the justification comes after the choice, not before.

There are some things in all of our lives that we can't change. Rather than being frustrated by them, choose to enjoy them, choose to embrace them. After all, perhaps spiritually (before we entered this plane of existence called humanity), we all chose the lives we now live, the circumstances we now have, and the difficulties we're now trying to overcome. Believe this to be true and our lives will transform.

Someone once said, "Maybe we're not human beings having a spiritual journey, maybe we're spiritual beings having a human journey." Choose to enjoy the journey.

" There are no limits in life.

History has already proven that. "

LIMIT
&
CONFINE

I got my first taste of word distinctions back in 11th grade. My English teacher, Mrs. Carrier, gave the class a several page listing of book titles. We were to choose a book from the list, read it, and write an essay on it. I asked Mrs. Carrier, "Are we limited to this list?" Mrs. Carrier said something like, "It's a pretty extensive list. You have lots of choices. No, you're not limited to this list. But I'll confine you to using this list."

She taught me a distinction by example. I hope good teachers like Mrs. Carrier have the opportunity to know some of the good they've shared with students throughout their years of teaching.

The word "limitation" has such a negative connotation. Limitations make us feel lesser than we are. They make us feel trapped. They imply there's an unbreakable barrier. I guess that's why there are so many inspirational quotations suggesting we surpass our limits. Even the music group 2Unlimited says, "No, no limits! We'll reach for the sky. No valley too deep, no mountain too high."

Being confined implies a temporary condition. All of us are confined at times. That's the nature of a changing environment in people's lives. Confinement isn't limiting.

Before the 1960s, we could have made two statements:

1) We're all limited to living on the planet Earth, and

2) We're all confined to living on the planet Earth.

Which one of these statements was true? Since we made it to the moon, the latter statement was the true statement. There was never any limit.

When we can choose between being limited and being confined, choose to be confined. It's nice to hear statements such as "Set no limits!" or "Break free of your limitations!" but what's more powerful is changing our vocabulary.

Limits make us feel we're the problem in a given circumstance. Confinements make us feel our environment is contributing to our circumstances and if we change the environment, we can change our confinement. For example, we can think, "I've never lifted 200 pounds. That's my limit." Or we can think, "I haven't yet been able to lift 200 pounds. That's my confinement." The next natural question is then, "How do I break through my confinement?"

There are no limits in life. History has already proven that. So why are we trying to break through our limits? Instead, let's just move out of our mental confinements.

FOCUS & PERSPECTIVE

Anthony Robbins says one of the ways to manage our state (control our emotions) is to change our focus. At any moment in time, there's an unlimited amount of information our brain can process. We must focus on a specific subset of that information. If we're feeling down, we're focusing on things that make us feel bad. If we change our focus, we're likely to change the way we're feeling. Changing our focus can be simple and very effective.

I see two main methods of focus. The first is to focus on something else besides the problem. For example, if we're feeling down about our job, we can take our focus into something completely different. We can think about family, our health or our upcoming vacation. We can go to a movie, talk to friends or listen to music. All of these things change our focus. This method postpones our feeling, which may sound negative but is sometimes useful. Although we put off the way we're feeling until later, later may be the better time to handle the way we feel.

The other method of changing our focus is to magnify specific areas of the issue at hand. Using the previous example of feeling down about work, we may focus on the things we do like about our job (there's always something!). We may think about people at work that we like. We may focus on an upcoming merger that will change things for the better. We change our focus to think about the possible good things in a particular issue. This alone may lead us to associate positive feelings with the issue.

Sometimes I think we need to go one step further than changing our focus and change our perspective. Charles Thompson says, "Never solve a problem from its original perspective." While changing our focus definitely helps us manage our state, I think changing perspective can help us manage our challenges – and there's always a different perspective to every challenge.

Still using the job example, changing our perspective may involve re-evaluating whether we're justified in feeling badly about our job. Maybe we've just been putting in extra hours the last couple of weeks because of a big account. Maybe the boss is noticing our extra effort and is considering us for a big promotion. Maybe with the extra commissions we're going to earn, we can buy our spouse that special present we've been wanting to get him or her. You see how changing our perspective is like changing the entire scene just by looking through a different lens?

Unless we change perspectives, we may be caught assuming something we shouldn't assume. Changing our perspective may allow us to dissolve those assumptions.

I heard the following spiritual example at one of my youth parliaments. A man said to God, I know you always walked beside me in my life through all the good times. I saw the footprints in the sand. I know you always walked beside me in the bad times. I saw the footprints then too. But I never saw any footprints during the really horrific struggles in my life. Why weren't you there for me?"

If we change our focus, we can think about how God was with us much of the time, that he may have been too busy in a select number of instances, or that he wanted us to grow in those very challenging times. When we hear God's answer, we realize the need to also change our perspective.

My child, you're right. I was there in the good times of your life and in the bad. When you had the worst times in your life, I was with you then too. You see, I carried you along when you couldn't walk. That's why you only saw one pair of footprints in the sand.

"Most people who say money is evil work eight hours or more a day for it. Does that mean they're working for evil?"

POOR, POVERTY, PROSPERITY WEALTH

 You can be poor and not live in poverty. You can be rich and live in extreme poverty. Being poor is a temporary economic condition. Poverty is a sinful way of thinking and being that degrades all aspects of your lifestyle.

Napoleon Hill, in his seminal book *Think and Grow Rich*, explains that true wealth begins with health, relationships, peace of mind, spirituality and other fruits of life. In fact, financial prosperity is the last thing that creates true wealth. Hill's book explains how to think and act in order to create wealth in all areas of our lives. Once we've done this, then we'll have escaped poverty thinking.

If we're in a poor economic condition but are applying the knowledge of Hill's book, then we're thinking out of poverty. We'll be giving away a percentage of our income, for example. We'll develop a plan to grow, confess our goals, and apply faith. These actions and the others described in the book, move us out of poverty and into prosperity.

Those who do have enormous bank accounts but don't live in prosperity are not difficult to recognize. They're cheap and count every dollar. They don't give money to causes they may believe in. They may not even believe in any causes. They'll spend five hours of their day looking for a bargain in order to save a dollar. They'll buy fancy cars to impress other people. They may have "status."

Status is buying things you don't need with money you don't have to impress people you don't like. If you've been poor, you may believe that people with status are wealthy. They're not. They may look wealthy to you but they're as far from wealth as those living in poverty.

Those who don't live in prosperity can also be recognized through poor health, poor attitude, and poor spiritual strength. The reason some people may be afraid of financial abundance is because they believe they'll lose their health, attitude, or spiritual stability as a result. That simply isn't true. Yes, true wealth means to have integrity, to have friends and family, to have your health and to appreciate life but that doesn't exclude economic prosperity. You can have it all.

Being poor isn't biblical. In fact, it's only the rich who create jobs for all the poor people. As elementary as this concept may be, most people don't grasp it. Robert Kiyosaki, the author of *Rich Dad, Poor Dad*, says, "The main reason people struggle financially is because they spent years in school but learned nothing about money. The result is people learn to work for money...but never learn how to have money work for them."

Most people who say money is evil work eight hours or more a day for it. Does that mean they're working for evil? The truth is, good people do good things with money, bad people do bad things with money. Are you a good person or a bad person?

If you're a good person, I suggest you read the books I have mentioned by Hill and Kiyosaki.

" *Life is simple.*

But it isn't easy. **"**

SIMPLE
&
EASY

This distinction may be simple to understand but not so easy to put into practice right away.

The opposite of simple is complicated. The opposite of easy is difficult. I think it's easier for people to recognize the difference between complicated and difficult than it is to recognize the difference between simple and easy. I'm not sure why that is.

Simplicity has to do with comprehension. Simple awareness increases our comprehension. Reading increases our ability to see things in life more simply. Rules are usually simple. Concepts are usually simple. Rituals are usually simple. Unfortunately, most things that are simple are difficult.

Ease has to do with effort and practice. We may have a skill or a talent that comes easily to us. Explaining how to perform a particular talent or employ a particular skill may not be very simple. What's easy for one person may be very difficult for another. The level of ease we associate with a particular task is usually based on experience. The amount of simplicity we associate with a particular idea may be based on intelligence. As we may know from life, intelligence is cheap, experience is expensive.

Then again, it depends on what kind of experience. It's easy to watch television. It's easy to be lazy. It's easy to stay comfortable. It's easy to not want to grow or try something new. It's easy to give up. Because it's also simple to do all these things, we get the worst of both worlds. Life is simple. But it isn't easy. Most things worth doing are simple and not easy.

You've probably heard that old saying, Keep It Simple, Stupid. I submit to you my own saying: Ease is To Avoid. K.I.S.S. your way to understanding, E.A.T. your way to success.

CONCLUSION FINALE

 Conclusion implies a summary – but there is none. Conclusion implies ending – but this is only the beginning. A conclusion may contain a moral, a motto or an undiscovered truth. I have already shown you enough morals, mottos and truths.

When I think of a finale, I think of *Pomp and Circumstance*. Do you hear the music? I hope this is a celebration! When I think of a finale, I feel excited. Is the adrenaline pumping within you?

Part of the reason I chose this distinction is because I just couldn't end the book on a regular distinction, could I? So I'll make this one short and sweet.

Don't conclude any aspects of your life – even if you fail in them. Transition out of them with a bang! Celebrate the transformation. Anticipate the way you'll use it in the future – and use it! Never forget anything. Someone once said, "Learning is remembering." (It's ironic how I don't remember who that is). Don't summarize your experience. Instead, use it as a reference and go back to it whenever you need to.

I hope you do that with this book. Use it. Live it. Teach it.

Refer back to it. Read it again. And if you want more, write to me and request a sequel. I would love to hear some of your distinctions too. I love you. God bless you.

Upcoming Titles

A Dictionary of Distinctions:
Volume II

A Dictionary of Distinctions
for Teenagers

A Dictionary of Distinctions
for Techies

A Dictionary of Distinctions
for Love & Marriage

A Dictionary of Distinctions
for Parents

A Dictionary of Distinctions
for Teachers

Have you thought of a distinction that isn't in this book? If you would like to submit a distinction of your own for possible use in an upcoming sequel, please e-mail it to Danish Ahmed at **danish@ordinarywords.com**

DISTINCTIONS
E-ZINE

If you would like to

receive chapters of dis-

tinctions that are not

in this book and that

are exclusive to our

Web site, subscribe to

the bi-weekly Distinctions e-Zine by visiting

www.ordinarywords.com.

Special Bonus

To thank you for purchasing and reading this book, I would like to send you a free Mini~Distinction™ Bookmark. Please fill out this order form for your free gift.

Name: _____

Company Name: _____

Street Address: _____

_____

City: _____ Province/State: _____

Postal/Zip Code: _____ Country: _____

E-Mail Address: _____

Phone Number: (____) _____

☐ **YES**, please subscribe me to the FREE Distinctions E-Zine. I have supplied my e-mail address above.

I would like **one** of the following **FREE** bookmarks:
☐ Statement & Expression   ☐ Suspend & Interrupt   ☐ Book & Script

I would also like to purchase:
(All amounts shown are in US dollars. Please remit US funds only.)

QTY	TITLE	PRICE
_____	6 bookmark set (Quick & Fast, Gift & Present, Complete & Whole, Statement & Expression, Suspend & Interrupt, Book & Script)	$4.95
_____	*A Dictionary of Distinctions: Volume I*	$14.95
_____	*A Dictionary of Distinctions: Volume II*	$14.95

$ _____ **Subtotal**
$ _____ **Shipping**
$ _____ **Taxes**
$ _____ **Total enclosed**

SHIPPING: Orders under $10 (including free orders), add $2
Orders $10+: add $5 for shipments to Canada,
$10 for the US, or $20 international
TAXES: Canadian residents, add 7% GST

Mail your check or money order to:
Ordinary Words ~ Extraordinary Power
34 Woodrow Ave. • Toronto, ON   M4C 5S2 • Canada
You can also place your order on-line at **www.ordinarywords.com**